TABLE OF CONTENTS

POISED

2 PRODUCE

FROM A MEDIOCRE TO A MASTERY MINDSET

NIKKI CHEREE

Editor: Angela Edwards – pearlygatespublishing.com

Formatting: Ya Ya Ya Creative – yayayacreative.com

ISBN No. 978-1-7335914-1-6

INTRODUCTION

As I pen this book, I can sense the passion and desire of the many of you who have made a quality decision to follow through on personal commitments and challenges that have been previously resting at bay. I am a proponent of transparency and practical teaching. This resource will help shift your mentality and propel you to the next level. This book is so important because it deals with your *mindset*. Being **Poised to Produce** is a state of mind.

A prevailing biblical passage is *"...as a man thinketh, so is he..."* (Proverbs 23:7). My challenge was to come up with a way to be transparent **and** motivate you to move beyond your current situation. You're already prepared and enabled with everything inside of you to create and deliver what God has purposed you to produce in the earth.

I want you to delve deeply into your state of mind so that you can come from a place of knowing **who** you are and **whose** you are. My deepest desire is that you move from a place of lack and mediocrity to mastery in every area of your life.

EXPOSE YOUR MINDSET

As an HR professional for almost 20 years, I spend a lot of one-on-one time with people. In this role and capacity, I have supported multi-billion-dollar businesses. The leaders of these businesses make decisions that affect the lives of everyone who reports to them, from the CEO down to front-line employees. What I realize is that some commonalities exist. People have asked me common questions and about things I deal with regarding people. They seek my wisdom and knowledge to determine best where I can make the most impact. My role is to allow them to see an alternative perspective. I help leaders inspire them and bring out the best in their teams as it relates to their performance.

Companies are in a state of constant change (restructuring, downsizing, war for talent, etc.).

People want to know, *"How is my performance being evaluated?" "How do I get to the next level?" "Why have I been overlooked?" "Is it just who you know?"* As I peel back the onion to formulate my responses, one of the first set of questions I ask them is, ***"What is your biggest accomplishment? Where do you place value in yourself?"***

People are becoming more introspective. Millennials want more meaningful work that aligns with their values and lifestyle. People want to find their purpose and match that with their careers. I want to understand what makes you tick and your motivation. Some are motivated by monetary reward, recognition, or a promotion. Others want to do what they do and leave. However, when we talk about getting to the next level and changing our mindset from mediocre to mastery, I want to understand the "why" behind the question. What is it that drives you and why are you attempting to do the things you are doing whether it's in the workplace, your community, at home, for our families, etc.? What is it that brings you value?

Let's use an example of someone on the job in Corporate America. It's common for performance to be the given, but when I start to peel back the onion, I realize there is a lot there—especially for people of color. We spend a lot of time trying to prove ourselves and live up to a set of standards that will continuously change. Once you reach a certain level of performance, the bar immediately rises. Then, you start to compare yourself to others in the same lane. The whole experience can be daunting! Everyone wants to know, *"How do I get a leg up? How do I move ahead of the masses?"*

When you look at performance distribution in general, 10% will be low performances, 25% will be top performers—where they are differentiated—and 65% will be in the middle, those who are consistently grinding. How do you make the step towards improvement? I am here to challenge your thought process concerning where you are and where you expect to be.

Let's start with **P.I.E.** (**P**erformance, **I**mage, and **E**xposure) in the workplace.

Performance is a given in any environment. When in school, you are expected to get good grades to earn a degree and get a good job. On the job, you are expected to perform to get a raise and be promoted to the next level. According to the organizational book, ***Empowering Yourself: The Organizational Game Revealed***, by Harvey Coleman, performance is only about 10% of a manager's assessment. It's the key to the entryway to get in the game. So, if you are performing on the level similar to everyone else, you will stay in the middle 65% ... with everyone else! Performance is 10% of the PIE.

Image is what other people think of you. It's your personal brand. Do you maintain a positive attitude? Do you lead with solutions to issues OR are you the person who only offers roadblocks? Your image is how you portray yourself. What is it about you that affects the environment around you? Image is 30% of the PIE.

Exposure is the next piece of the PIE. Who knows about you? Does your community know about you? Does the next layer up in the organization know about you? Does your target audience really know you and what you have to offer? When you think about it, exposure is 60% of the PIE. And if you are moving from a mediocre mindset to a mastery mindset, you must ensure that you are focused on getting where you want to be.

So, what now? Your image or brand is 30% of the PIE. What speaks for you when you are not in the room? Are you speaking or is someone else speaking for you? Is there confidence when you walk by or is there a question mark? Who knows the impact of what you have done?

I realize that as a woman of color, I had to claw my way through to get a piece of the PIE in a male-dominated industry. I had to do double the work to get to the next level. However, let me challenge your thought process by stating the following:

"What you produce should be as unto God."

How coincidental is it that your performance (which represents 10% of the PIE) is symbolic of the tithe? Like the tithe, your performance is your reasonable service. If you think that you are on your job, own that business, or are a leader in the church and will impact lives but is **NOT** as unto God, then that's mediocre. Mastery comes from the master. When we give God our tenth, what He does is blesses the other 90%! For example, with your image, you must know who you are and whose you are. Who do you represent in the marketplace? There should be no shame in your game. When people see you, they should see the likeness of Christ. Why? Because it is a platform—a means to an end.

I am flipping the script on the biggest piece of the PIE because favor is not fair. We will replace exposure with the "favor of the Lord." When you realize you are walking in the grace and unmerited favor of God which He bestows on you, then you can act boldly without hesitation. When you pray with specificity to the Lord, He will whisper in your ear that you already have the resources needed, instruct you on who needs to be moved, and orchestrate what needs to happen. God gives the increase and seed to the sower!

EMBRACE YOUR PROCESS

*P*eople can become limited by the box of mediocrity and become conditioned to believe that there really is a ceiling or that they've reached their best when they can pay all the bills. At an early age, we learn that practice makes perfect or to become satisfied with taking on a plethora of things that reduce us to "Jack of all trades and master of none." I am here to challenge whether or not that is true mastery.

The definition of the word **poised** is: *1. (of a person) composed, dignified, and self-assured; 2. Being in balance or equilibrium.* The word poised is an adjective, and an adjective is a modifier of a noun (person, place, or thing). In this case, it's you and me. We are the noun that is being modified by being poised. That means we walk in composure and dignity. We walk with self-assurance because we represent our

Heavenly Father. If we represent Him, we can walk in confidence. Some synonyms for self-assurance are **polished, grace, and refinement.** Those are not terms we use with people who are mediocre or who haphazardly bump into a blessing they're unable to handle. In every area of your life, your mindset can always be on mastery because you know what the end is. The end is victory! You have the confidence to know that based on scripture:

"Remember those early days after you first saw the light? Those were the hard times! Kicked around in public, targets of every kind of abuse—some days it was you, other days your friends. If some friends went to prison, you stuck by them. If some enemies broke in and seized your goods, you let them go with a smile, knowing they couldn't touch your real treasure. Nothing they did bothered you, nothing set you back.

So, don't throw it all away now. You were sure of yourselves then. It's still a sure thing! But you need to stick it out, staying with God's plan so you'll be there for the promised completion. It won't be long now. He's on the way; He'll show up most any minute.

But anyone who is right with me thrives on loyal trust; if he cuts and runs, I won't be very happy. But we're not quitters who lose out. Oh, no! We'll stay with it and survive, trusting all the way."
–Hebrews 10:32-39 (MSG)

I encourage you to create that balance and do it with grace so that we can **produce**. The definition of the word produce (which is a verb) is: *1. To bring into existence; give rise to; cause; 2. To bring into existence by intellectual or creative ability.* So, we now have a noun being modified by an adjective—how we accomplish this thing which is to produce. The Creator has already implanted inside of you what you need to create! This is exciting because when you put poised and produce together, here is what you get:

You are composed, dignified, and self-assured to bring that business, job, ministry, and service—whatever that is for you—into existence by your intellectual or creative ability and, therefore, maximizing your piece of the PIE (Performance, Image, and Exposure).

I've given you a lot, but there is more. I am going to keep building on this to ensure you understand, so let's take it a step further. There are three typical phases of progression for a new employee to progress through their career. They are:

1. **Learning Phase**

   The learning phase is where you can rely on your education, training, and practice because you're a novice and don't really know all that you have to know. You can experience stops and starts and may even fail at times, but it's okay because there may have been some form of cushion in place for you. At this point, you are soaking it all in, getting all the knowledge you need so that you can perform on a consistent basis. Some might consider this a mediocre phase, perhaps, if your mindset is focused on "knowing what I need to know so I can get the work done." We will talk about how to elevate that thinking later.

2. Testing and Modeling Phase

The testing and modeling phase is where most people stop because, after all, practice makes perfect! You can now do "it" on your own and are no longer learning. You can apply knowledge to real-life applications. You have become comfortable with doing it on your own. Perhaps you're now coming up with new ideas and performing at a high level. You may have even gotten recognition for your efforts. You have made it through tests and trials and proved to others what you can do and what you are made of. Remember: The bar has already been set for you by someone else and you may find yourself giving in and accepting that bar. That is mediocre.

3. Teaching or Releasing Phase

At this point, you are the pro in the place and can teach others. You may have a broader impact than just your immediate surroundings. Perhaps you are doing something at a community level. Maybe you're operating outside of your team or have a couple of other teams that you're able to impact. The teaching or releasing phase is a pivotal moment because once you can teach something, you consider yourself to be an expert and can become complacent. However, even in being an expert, you can still be mediocre. The pivotal moment is when you decide to step out like Jabez and ask the Lord to expand your territory. The alternative way of thinking would be to excel where you are and remain at the top of the food chain in your circle. If you are the highest rung on the ladder in the circle you are in, you need a new circle.

How many of us allow ourselves to come outside of "I've reached the top"? Are you willing to step out and start the process all over again because you have a mastery mindset and know the impact you have in an organization? If you can do one, why not another? The Word says that *"one can put a thousand to flight and 2, ten thousand"* (Deuteronomy 32:30). How many more can you impact if you step outside of the box created for you? **That's mastery.**

My message here is straightforward: I am trying to create ways of expression and instances that will sink into your heart through real-life examples. I want them to stir your spirit, to the point you realize that if people who have the shining accolades and fancy words are not impacting the hearts and minds of others, it all means **nothing** if they have no effectual impact! Mastery is when you produce answers and provide solutions that change the hearts and minds of those in both your immediate and distant circles. That's the realm of mastery. You can achieve mastery in your learning phase, in your testing and modeling phase, and certainly in your teaching and releasing phase because it's a mindset. Now you know what the end-game is: **VICTORY!**

My name is Nikki Cheree. Nikki means "victory of the people." Cheree means "darling or beloved one." Everyone reading this book is beloved. As for me, I have been through hell and back, so I know how to go through to get to. If I can do it, you can do it.

Joseph is a classic example in the Bible of a mastery mindset. No matter where he was or what stage of life he was in, he was the cream of the crop and more was given to him. He was a conduit, and he excelled. You can, too, by the renewing of your mind. I want to make the life examples shared here relevant so that you can get all that you need. Deuteronomy 8:17-18 (MSG) speaks of you beginning to produce in this way:

"If you start thinking to yourselves,
"I did all this. And all by myself. I'm rich. It's all
mine!" Well, think again. Remember that GOD,
your God, gave you the strength to produce all this
wealth to confirm the covenant that He promised
to your ancestors—as it is today."

Are you a conduit so that the kingdom of the Lord can be established on the earth? As it was promised then, so be it today. Your purpose is to help people. Your passion is how you execute it.

If you think in terms of mastery—the "what" and the "how" you get it done—then it will take you to a different level when you understand why are doing what you're doing. God created you and said, *"You are poised for it."* It doesn't mean the attacks of the enemy won't come against you or that the fiery darts won't sting, but you get up with grace. You walk in balance, are sure-footed, and your feet walk in peace. No weapon that is formed against you will prosper. You are poised for this because you know the end-game. You are positioned for this now. No matter what stage of the game you are in, you've already won!

Let's review some practical examples of "good" versus "mastery":

- You come home and make a good dinner for your family. Your bellies are full, and that's great! However, when it's **mastery**, you take your children out for a 5-course meal at a 5-star restaurant as a treat to them.

- When you exercise for three weeks so you can lose five pounds, that's good—but that's not mastery. When I create a health and wellness plan for my family and me so that what I take in reflects what comes out and am consciously aware of our health and well-being spiritually, mentally, and emotionally—***THAT'S* mastery**.

- When I'm going on vacation and staying at a Motel 6, that may be what I need to do at the moment. That's good, but it's not *Four Seasons* **mastery**.

Those are just a few common illustrations of how we can frame our mindset. Our reference frame of mind is so important. I encourage you to examine every area of your life in the same fashion (family, health, job/career, finances, and ministry). Are you a conduit?

God gives seed to the sower, but not if you are constipated. You've got to release it! You are expected to produce and do it with grace and refinement. What you produce is your gift to God and should be released. Mastery is about recognizing that **HE** is the source. **HE** provides the seed. It's up to you to master the process to harvest and expand the seed like the story of the talents in the Bible. Are you going to bring back just the one talent He gave you or will you multiply through your intellect and creative mindset?

You will create different ways and through multiple revenue streams to sow through both time and resources. When you put your hands to the plow, it should be with a purpose. You understand the "why," the "how," and the "what" platforms to get you there. Rest assured that God will provide a way for you to accomplish the task.

EXPAND YOUR TERRITORY

In this last section, let's discuss the differences that transform regarding **Poised to Produce**. We referenced the why, what, and how. I want to give you some wisdom nuggets of how I have been able to progress and climb the corporate ladder.

It was a challenge to become successful in this arena. However, I accepted that challenge a long time ago. I already knew this when I was an abused young child who used to play in the closet with my imaginary friends. I created a frame of reference that said, *"This is **not** where I will end up!"* I created a businesswoman in that closet. I created an actress in that closet. God maintained and kept my mind in that closet. Today, I have a manifestation of what I saw back then as a nine-year-old abuse victim. Some of the nuggets I have learned will help you shift from a mediocre mindset to one of mastery:

- ***Be willing to step into new territory.*** We have so many people who can do a lot of virtually everything with gifts and talents. You must know when to use them. They should all be used to accomplish that one thing God purposed you to do. When you achieve it, then be willing to step into new territory with that gift.

- ***Apply the proven methods you learned from level to level.*** *(i.e., three phases of progression).* There are principles that you practice and achieve mastery in. Your state of mind cultivates it as you evolve from knowledge to wisdom. You must know when to apply it. You must know and discern the audience and understand the right time to strike strategically.

- ***Sow seeds now for later harvest.*** It doesn't matter how big the seeds are. Impart into someone else who is struggling beside you and help them along. It doesn't have to be money. When you sow now, you can expect a harvest later. It will come back to you. The seed is working, even when you forgot about it. Someone else will water and nourish it, and God will bless and increase it.

- *Maintain an unrelenting spirit of excellence in everything you do. Don't "half-do" anything.* If you are the type of person who has to say "YES!" to everyone and it gets half-done, say "NO!" and be okay with your "No!" And don't explain it. It's a 'no' because it's a 'no'! You understand why. You cannot afford to half-do or misuse the gift God gave to you because everything you do is as unto Him.

- *Anticipate risks.* You are going to be tested. Are you prepared for the tests? Do you have a plan of action? For example, do you have an emergency fund? When you are prepared, it will make your life easier.

- *Manage setbacks.* Don't be afraid. Setbacks don't stop you; they just slow you down. Don't give up, cave in, or quit. Manage the setback. Recognize the setbacks for what they are, learn the lesson, and keep it moving.

- *Increase your impact.* Once you have gotten good and can teach, the best way to increase impact is to duplicate the process. Teach others how to do what you do. Your gift will make room for you. Imitation is, indeed, the best form of flattery!

- ***Stay true to God and yourself.*** Don't worry about what people will think. Remove the mask and enjoy being who you are. Remain who you are in every setting by bringing your whole self to every opportunity.

- ***Be in position.*** A master is ready for the opportunity to shift and move. Once blessings come your way, you will be ready—not trying to **GET** ready. When the ball is thrown to you, you must catch it and be in a position to receive the opportunity.

- ***Stay relevant.*** Stay relevant now and remain relevant in the future. Make sure what you produce today is of value! Think ahead on how you can modify, elevate, or evolve for tomorrow.

- ***Shape your frame of reference.*** Bust open the ceiling that puts you in a box! There is no such thing as a box when you have a mastery mindset. SPEAK FAITH! Leverage resources that feed you positive affirmations and shape you for success. Build your personal brand. After all, no one can promote you better than YOU! Surround yourself with positive influences that are where you want to be.

• *Be consistent in daily practice.* We are all familiar with the wash cycle (wash, rinse, dry). I will share the parallels of the wash cycle and how you position yourself via this audio link: https://drive.google.com/file/d/1uRcyN02h6 CQOsMwfEy1bOlVKIyEe0xYE/view?usp=dri vesdk.

BONUS MATERIAL:
WASH CYCLE OUTLINE

1. **Wash**

   a. Soak

      i. Pretreat

      ii. Loosen particles

      iii. Education

      iv. Pour in all cleaning agents

      v. Prepare for your cleansing

      vi. Gather your resources

      vii. Training/Tools

      viii. Sit/Learn/Watch

      ix. No agitation or activation yet

      x. Saturation in the Word/Presence of God—sowing seeds in prayer

      xi. You envision what clean will look like

   b. Wash cycle begins

   c. Agitation—starting to step out in gifts and doing

   d. Bad habits are being scrubbed

   e. Go through some pulling, wringing, stretching

   f. New ground; make some mistakes, but the whole time, the water (Holy Spirit) is all around you

   g. Making some noise; there is a buzz

2. Rinse

   a. Add in fabric softener

   b. Bad habits are falling off

   c. New countenance—you can see yourself "like new."

   d. Fresh water

   e. Softener —> Begin to discern and know your audience

   f. Confidence in your skill because you have been the "conditioning agent" of the Holy Spirit to build skill in you.

3. Spin

   a. Whirlwind experience

   b. Allow your opportunities to take over

c. You're on top of your game, but adversaries are watching and all around you.

d. Fast pace —> Time of expansion and squeezing out of heavy, dead weight. You can't take it with you into the "new you."

e. Ready to perform at a high level.

4. Dry

a. Ready to wear

b. You are an example

c. The heat of the tests and trials shows your resilience.

d. The fabric of your life has been woven to sustain the pressures of life and bounce back.

e. Have the ability to maintain your shape

f. Anointing has sealed and locked in despite the tossing and turning in the dryer.

    g. Press/Iron

    i. Maximum heat and pressure

    ii. Eliminate the wrinkles

iii.   You are distinguishing yourself and YOUR brand

iv.   Shows your flair and style (SWAG)

v.   Garment (Anointing) flows when you wear it from the inside out

vi.   You are new; old things are passed away

vii.   Aroma/Scent of success all over you

viii.   Starch/Finisher—Crisp and Poised

I hope that one of the examples shared has given you a renewed sense of purpose. My goal is to inspire you to activate something inside of you in any area of your life. Make a commitment today by declaring:

"I am going to move from mediocrity to mastery because I know who I am and who I represent! I make a quality decision today to never be the same!"

Remember: You are **"Poised to Produce"**— and someone is waiting for **YOU!**